D0461606

MAR    2010

A FIRE SAFETY BOOK

# FIREBOY

## TO THE RESCUE!

### BY EDWARD MILLER

HOLIDAY HOUSE / NEW YORK

THANKS TO THE FDNY FIRE SAFETY
EDUCATION UNIT FOR ITS EXPERT REVIEW
OF THIS BOOK AND FOR THE FINE WORK IT DOES
EDUCATING CHILDREN ABOUT FIRE SAFETY.
—E. M.

PRINTED AND BOUND IN OCTOBER 2009 IN JOHOR BAHRU, JOHOR, MALAYSIA, AT TIEN WAH PRESS.
WWW.HOLIDAYHOUSE.COM
FIRST EDITION
1 3 5 7 9 10 8 6 4 2

LIBRARY OF CONGRESS CATALOGING-IN-PUBLICATION DATA

MILLER, EDWARD, 1964–
FIREBOY TO THE RESCUE! : A FIRE SAFETY BOOK /
BY EDWARD MILLER. — 1ST ED.
P. CM.
ISBN 978-0-8234-2222-7 (HARDCOVER)
1. FIRE PREVENTION—JUVENILE LITERATURE. 2. FIRES—SAFETY
MEASURES—JUVENILE LITERATURE. I. TITLE.
TH9148.M54 2009
628.9'2—DC22
2009014481

THE BLACK-AND-WHITE PHOTO ON PAGE ELEVEN IS FROM THE AUTHOR'S PERSONAL COLLECTION.

THE IMAGE ON PAGE FIFTEEN, "BENJAMIN FRANKLIN, THE FIREMAN" BY CHARLES WASHINGTON WRIGHT,
IS REPRODUCED WITH THE PERMISSION OF
THE SMITHSONIAN NATIONAL MUSEUM OF AMERICAN HISTORY.

Visit www.edmiller.com for activities for kids and materials for teachers and librarians that accompany this book.

Join the Edward Miller Fan Club to receive e-mail announcements of new books, projects, and contests. It's free!

DON'T EVER
call 911 if it's not
an emergency—false alarms
can endanger people who
really need help!
FIREBOY,
HELP!

# TO THE RESCUE

AT THE FIREHOUSE AN ALARM RINGS, AND THE FIREFIGHTERS ARE READY TO GO.

QUICKLY THEY JUMP INTO THE FIRE ENGINE. THERE IS NO TIME TO WASTE!

OOOEEEOOOEEE

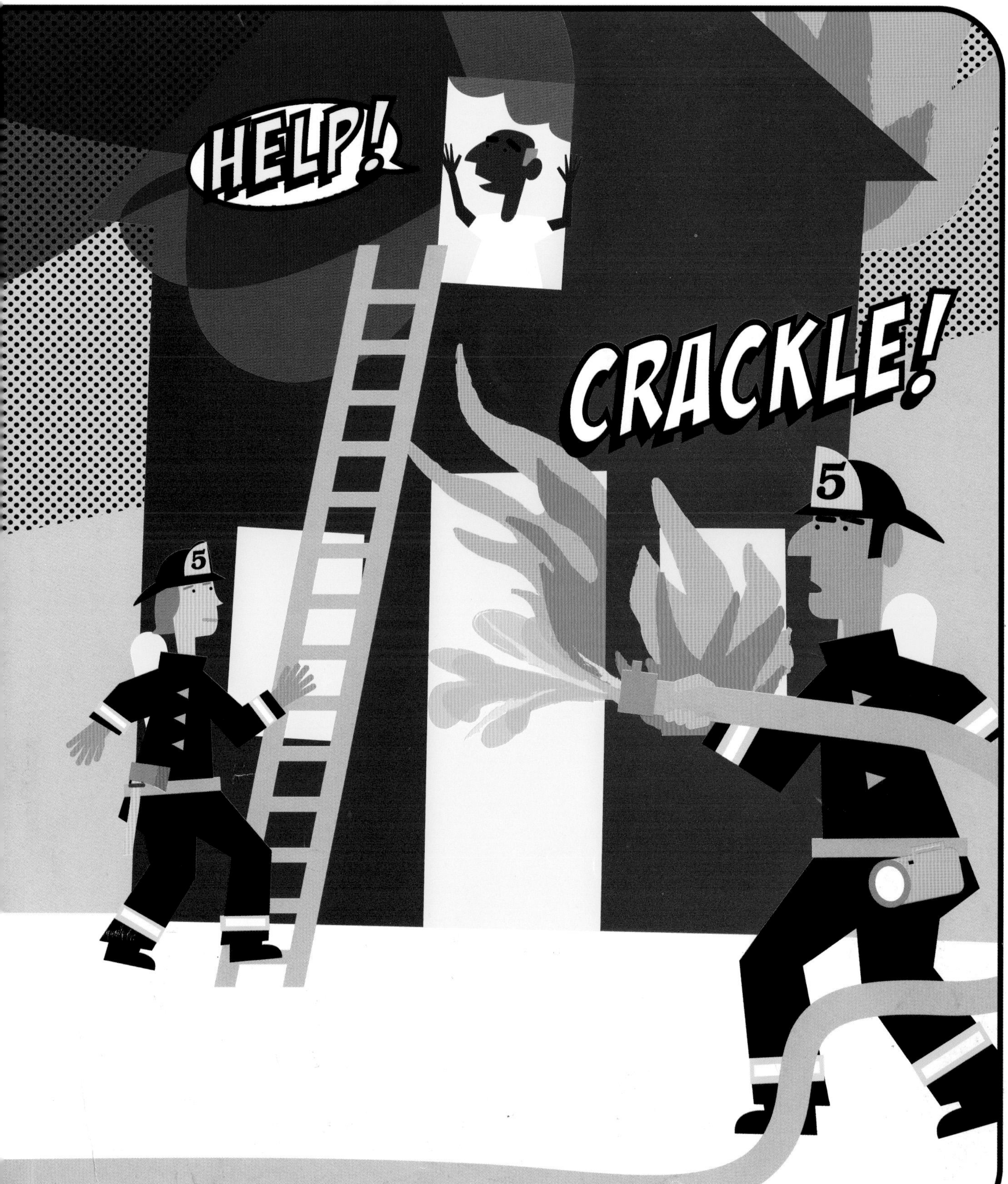
HELP!
CRACKLE!
5
5

**I**F YOUR CLOTHES CATCH ON FIRE . . .

# STOP

WHERE YOU ARE,
DON'T RUN . . .

# DROP

TO THE GROUND . . .

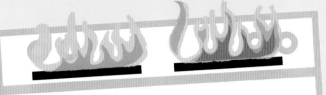

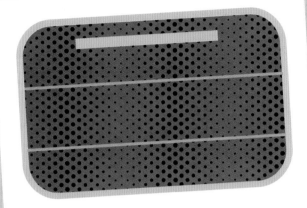

**STOVES**

**CiGARETTES**

**SPACE HEATERS**

**OUTLETS**

October 9 is FIRE PREVENTION DAY. It marks the day of the Great Chicago Fire that burned down a large part of the city in 1871.

STOVES
KEEP THE STOVE CLEAR OF THINGS THAT CAN BURN, SUCH AS OVEN MITTS. KEEP POT HANDLES TURNED INWARD SO THE POTS ARE NOT ACCIDENTALLY KNOCKED OVER. DON'T GET CLOSE TO THE FLAMES.
If a fire starts, get an adult! DON'T try to put the fire out yourself.
BLAST!
AND...

# BURN!

### SPACE HEATERS
KEEP SPACE HEATERS AT LEAST 3 FEET AWAY FROM THINGS THAT CAN BURN. REMIND AN ADULT TO TURN OFF SPACE HEATERS BEFORE LEAVING THE HOUSE OR GOING TO BED.

### LAMPS
LIGHTBULBS CAN GET VERY HOT. *DON'T DRAPE CLOTHES OVER A LAMPSHADE.* THE FABRIC CAN HEAT UP AND CATCH ON FIRE.

### CIGARETTES
CIGARETTES ARE THE LEADING CAUSE OF FATAL FIRES IN THE U.S. THEY ARE HAZARDOUS TO YOUR HEALTH, TOO!

TELL SMOKERS TO USE DEEP ASHTRAYS AND NEVER SMOKE IN BED OR FALL ASLEEP WITH A LIT CIGARETTE IN THEIR HAND.

# IGNITE!

# SAFETY DEVICES

A FIRE CAN HAPPEN IN ANY HOME, SO IT'S IMPORTANT TO HAVE THESE SAFETY DEVICES IN CASE A FIRE STARTS. *THEY CAN SAVE YOUR LIFE!*

BEEP! BEEP! BEEP!

**SMOKE ALARM**
A DEVICE THAT SETS OFF AN ALARM WHEN IT SENSES SMOKE

**FIRE EXTINGUISHER**
A DEVICE FILLED WITH FOAM OR WATER THAT CAN PUT OUT A SMALL FIRE

# ESCAPE PLAN

EVERY HOUSE SHOULD HAVE A ESCAPE PLAN SO EVERYONE KNOWS HOW TO GET OUT SAFE IF THERE IS A FIRE.

Check smoke alarms every month to make sure they are working. Replace the batteries twice a year.

As you le each room, sh door to prev fire from spre

BEEP! BEEP! BEEP!

BEEP! BEEP! BEEP!